Birds of Houston

Birds

of

Houston

B.C. Robison

Photographs by

John L. Tveten

Rice University Press

Houston, Texas

Published in association

with the Houston Museum

of Natural Science

Copyright 1990
by Rice University Press
All rights reserved
First Edition, 1990
Printed in USA
Requests for permission
to reproduce material
from this work
should be addressed to
Rice University Press
Post Office Box 1892
Houston, Texas 77251

Library of Congress Catalog
Card Number 90-53175
ISBN 0-89263-303-4 clothbound
ISBN 0-89263-304-2 paperbound

Library of Congress
Cataloging-in-Publication Data
Robison, B. C., 1946–
    Birds of Houston / B.C.
Robison ; photographs by John
L. Tveten.—1st ed.
        p.   cm.
    ISBN 0-89263-303-4 :
$22.50.—ISBN 0-89263-304-2
(pbk.) : $10.95
    1. Birds—Texas—
Houston—
Identification.   I. Tveten, John
L.   II. Title.
QL684.T4R63   1990
598.29764′1411—dc20
                            90-53175
                            CIP

Contents

ix   Acknowledgments

1   Introduction

11   Northern Mockingbird
14   Blue Jay
16   Ring-billed Gull
18   House Sparrow

21   DOVES
21   Rock Dove
22   Mourning Dove
22   Inca Dove
22   Ringed Turtle-Dove

27   WOODPECKERS
28   Red-bellied Woodpecker
28   Pileated Woodpecker
28   Downy Woodpecker
29   Yellow-bellied Sapsucker
29   Red-headed Woodpecker
29   Northern Flicker

39   BLACKBIRDS
39   American Crow
40   Great-tailed Grackle
40   Common Grackle
41   European Starling
41   Brown-headed Cowbird
42   Red-winged Blackbird

52   Northern Cardinal

55   BIRDS OF THE SUMMER SKY
55   Purple Martin
56   Chimney Swift
56   Common Nighthawk

62   Cedar Waxwing
64   Killdeer
66   Northern Harrier

69   HAWKS
69   Red-tailed Hawk
70   Red-shouldered Hawk

74   American Kestrel
76   Eastern Meadowlark
78   Mississippi Kite
80   Loggerhead Shrike

83   BIRDS OF THE WOODLANDS
83   Carolina Wren
83   Carolina Chickadee
83   Tufted Titmouse
84   Ruby-crowned Kinglet
84   Orange-crowned Warbler
84   Yellow-rumped Warbler
85   Blue-gray Gnatcatcher

95   HERONS AND EGRETS
95   Great Egret
95   Cattle Egret
96   Yellow-crowned Night-Heron
97   Green-backed Heron

102   American Robin
104   Lesser Snow Goose
106   Turkey Vulture

109   O W L S
109   Eastern Screech-Owl
109   Barn Owl

115   Ruby-throated Hummingbird
118   Scissor-tailed Flycatcher
120   Barn Swallow
122   Eastern Bluebird
125   Brown Thrasher
127   Brown Creeper

Acknowledgments

Every book, even a modest volume such as this, has many authors. Over the years I have had the honor and pleasure of knowing many people who in some way, whether large or small, have contributed to this book. For their support, inspiration, and companionship, I would like to gratefully acknowledge the following people: Kuyk Logan, Frank Fisher, Jr., C. H. Ward, T. Ben Feltner, Linda Miller Feltner, Larry White, Jim Blackburn, Jr., Garland Kerr, Lynn Ashby, Ernie Williamson, Edith Masquelette, Ron Sass, Paul Harcombe, Ted Eubanks, Jr., Jim Morgan, Noel Pettingell, Ron Grimes, Mary and Edward Hannigan, and John and Princie Chapman.

Special thanks go to the editors of Rice University Press, Susan Fernandez, Susan Bielstein, and Fred von der Mehden, and to their staff for their patience and encouragement during the writing of this book.

Generous support from Phillips Petroleum Company has helped make possible the color illustrations.

I also owe a special debt of gratitude to John Tveten, who provided the excellent photographs for this guide. John's "Nature Trails" column in the *Houston Chronicle* inspired me to create the "Texas Naturalist" for the *Houston Post.*

Furthermore, I would never have attempted nature writing if my parents, Mr. and Mrs. B. C. Robison, Jr., of Houston, had not instilled in me at an early age a respect for nature and a love of wildlife. To them I am especially grateful. Finally, to my wife, Middy Randerson, whose understanding and patience carried me through many months of writing, this book is affectionately dedicated.

Birds of Houston

INTRODUCTION

Wherever you see birds in the city—in parks or woodlands, on power lines or in parking lots, in ditches or in the sky—they are the natural soul of the urban landscape. They enhance the city and the lives of those who watch them. Observing birds, however, can arouse mixed feelings. To me an unidentified bird is an annoyance. If I see a bird, I want to know what it is. I suspect that most people feel the same way. This little field guide is for Houston city-dwellers and visitors who want to learn to identify the common birds that we see throughout the year in and around Houston.

Birdwatching as a pastime is said to be exceeded in popularity in this country only by gardening. I know people who will hop into a car and drive three hundred miles on a moment's notice to see a rare species that has unexpectedly been sighted. There are others who frequently take trips out through the countryside, or who rush down to High Island or Rockport during a migrant-concentrating rainstorm in April, constantly adding to their "life list," the record of all the species that a birder has ever identified in the field. There are devotees who may take a lengthy trip or two each year to Big Bend or southeastern Arizona or Mexico or some other birding "hot spot" in order to build their entire vacation around a birdwatching adventure.

For these birders there is a variety of excellent and comprehensive field guides. Such guides are for the birdwatchers who want information like the extent of the summer range of the vermilion flycatcher or the difference between a Sprague's pipit and a water pipit. But not everyone wants to know that much. During the years that I have been writing the "Texas Naturalist" column for the *Houston Post,* so many people have asked me about the birds they routinely observe in town that I came to realize there was no guidebook primarily for the beginning birder who wants to learn to identify birds in Houston. Some of us need simple information like the name of the big black bird with the long tail that struts around the grocery store parking lot or of the pretty golden-brown birds with black masks that flock to the pyracantha bush in winter.

There is inevitably a certain arbitrariness in selecting birds for a field guide like this one with a rather narrow focus. I have chosen the fifty-five birds that I consider the most common and the most likely to be seen year round by the observant city resident. Another author could have picked a somewhat different list, but I suspect the two would be greatly similar. There were several criteria for selection. One was population numbers. I don't consider sparrows and cowbirds and grackles particularly interesting birds, but they are abundant and widespread throughout the city and they are therefore included. Other birds are less numerous but are easily seen, full of personality, or just fun to watch; these species include such urban favorites as the mockingbird, the blue jay, the cardinal, and the woodpeckers. Still other birds, like the great egret, the cattle egret, and the yellow-crowned night heron, might be even less common. But because of their size or their exotic appearance or their tendency to inhabit open, visible areas, you will frequently see them. The migratory songbirds, like the warblers that pass through briefly each spring and fall, were not included. These birds are often difficult to see and to identify, and they belong more to the trophy list of the experienced birder.

In this book John Tveten and I have provided for each bird a color photograph, a brief description of its appearance and behavior, and—for quick reference—a summary of the primary field marks of the adult bird. The photographs show the birds in their adult plumage, which often varies from that of the juveniles. This field-mark summary includes not only identifying features of the bird but also the habitat in which you will most often see the bird, the time of year it is most commonly observed, and its distinctive behavioral traits. For habitat I have given general descriptions rather than specific locations, which may change over time. Birds will persist around a given area for a while, but they will also move on. In dealing with seasonal occurrence, I have given the time of year that the bird is most likely to be seen in the Houston area. Birds can also occur less commonly at other times of the year, but for simplicity I have omitted those occurrences. I have also omitted technical terms when describing a bird's appearance. Most terms are self-explanatory; others used are "crown" (top of the head), "nape" (lower back of the head), and "length" (average length from tip of beak to tip of tail). I have included descriptions of song only for those species for which recognition of song might be of value in identification.

The Fundamentals of Birdwatching

Like playing the piano or baking bread, identifying birds is a skill that improves with practice and weakens with neglect. And like other skills, successful birdwatching depends on the steady adherence to a few fundamentals. They are: 1) proper use of the field guide,

2) correct technique in observation, and 3) persistence.

It may seem unnecessary to suggest ways to use an apparently simple book. After all, don't you just take the book outdoors and flip through the pages until you see the illustration of the bird that you are looking at? Actually that is how a field guide—any field guide—should *not* be used.

Years ago professional birding guide T. Ben Feltner of Seattle taught me the proper way to use a birdwatching field guide. Feltner's advice was simple but effective: use the book before birdwatching, not during. Study the book first, read through it leisurely, look over the illustrations, and get a strong general impression of the bird. Don't worry at first about memorizing each tiny detail of the bird's appearance, but develop a sense of the bird's shape and primary identifying features. Often you can identify a bird on the basis of one or two key features.

Above all, don't try to look at the bird and the book at the same time. This is a common mistake that beginning birders make. The result is that you don't see the bird or use the book very well. Of course you will want to have your book handy when birdwatching. Once you have seen the bird as well as conditions permit, refer to the guide to confirm the bird's identity. At this point you can review the finer points of the bird's plumage and structural characteristics that you have seen.

Finally, don't become a slave to the field guide. The book is an essential piece of birding equipment, but it is not infallible. Birds, like all creatures, show natural variation in appearance among individuals of a species. There will be occasions when the bird you see in the field may not resemble precisely the bird in the book. The field guide is just what it claims to be—a guide. Don't expect it to present an exact representation of every bird you will ever see.

Once you have become familiar with the field guide, your next task is simple in theory but often difficult to carry out: get a good look at the bird. If you can't see the bird properly, all the glossy field guides and expensive binoculars in the world won't make a birder out of you. By "good look" at the bird I don't mean simply seeing it up close and in bright sunlight. Don't just aimlessly watch the bird. Learn to look at birds with a sense of purpose; make an effort to discern specific features that will aid you in identification. Go through a mental checklist. Look for the following characteristics:

- the color of the bird's back, chest, belly, flank, rump, throat, and wings
- the shape of the tail and beak
- special features, such as throat and cheek patches, eye-rings, face masks, wing bars, moustaches, crown stripes, and eye color
- the bird's silhouette in flight and its style of flying
- the bird's overall shape.

Don't expect to see everything on every bird you look at; you won't. The bird may be too far away, or the light may be poor, or the bird simply won't stay in one place. Expect difficulties like this. They will be your constant birdwatching companions.

Just concentrate on getting the best look at the bird that you can. Consult the field guide later. Make written notes if you find that helpful, including the location and date as well as important field marks.

Learn to associate birds and their habitats. Although

field marks are essential to bird identification, a bird is more than just a feathered collection of stripes or streaks. Noting the natural surroundings of a bird can rapidly narrow your possibilities. For example, if you see a flock of dark birds on the grass, you'll know immediately that they have to be grackles, starlings, or cowbirds, or, in winter, robins. A long-tailed brown bird in the underbrush of your yard or in woodlands will most likely be a brown thrasher.

Bird behavior is often an excellent clue to identification, especially when you can't observe specific field marks. You may not be able to see the wing bars on a certain long-winged bird flying way up high, but the jerky, leisurely flight pattern will identify it as a common nighthawk. You may be too far away to see the eye mask and red wing spots, but a flock of buttery-brown birds flying in a quick, tight formation onto a loquat tree will tell you that they are cedar waxwings.

Finally, learn the seasons of the year that birds move into and out of the Houston area. Some birds, like the mockingbird and blue jay, are found all year. Others, like the ruby-crowned kinglet and yellow-bellied sapsucker, live in the area mostly in winter. And still other birds, like the Mississippi kite and chimney swift, are birds of summer. Knowing when to expect certain birds as well as where will serve you greatly in identifying them.

One of the keys to successful birding is simply to do it often. If all you ever do is take field guide and binoculars in hand and go to Hermann Park once every summer, your birding skills will never mature. Each time you see a bird in town try to identify it, even if you're not close to it and you don't have your binoculars. The best birdwatchers are people who watch birds at every opportunity. I know birders who travel somewhere every weekend of the year to see birds, who birdwatch on vacations and business trips, and who go on every organized field trip they can. Not all of us have that level of interest or that much time to devote to birding, but we can often birdwatch in the city—such opportunities present themselves every day. Doing yard work, going to the store, taking the children to school, or walking through a parking lot will bring you in contact with our urban bird life. Birdwatching does not have to be a big production; let birds happen to you.

Buying Binoculars

In addition to a field guide and a firm commitment to learning birds and spending time watching them, the birdwatcher needs a good pair of binoculars. They are, however, expensive, so it helps to know something about them before you buy.

Binoculars have two important features: magnification and brightness. Magnification enlarges the image of an object and brings it in close to the observer. Brightness results from the amount of light transmitted through the lenses to the observer's eye; it is as important to the quality of binoculars as magnification. Both features depend on the size, arrangement, and quality of the lenses and on their optical surfaces.

All binoculars are designated by a pair of numbers, such as 7×35, 8×40, or 10×50, among several other combinations. The first of these numbers is the magnification. A magnification of 10 means that a bird 100 yards away will appear 10 yards away (100 divided by 10). The greater the magnification, the closer the bird appears. The second of these numbers is the diameter of the objective lens, and it is a measure of brightness. The objective lens makes up the large end of the binoculars, the end facing the object being observed. Since this lens gathers in the image, its diameter determines the brightness of what you see.

As magnification increases, however, brightness decreases. For example, a 7-power binoculars admits more light than a 10-power pair, if other factors such as lens quality and objective lens diameter are equal. Sufficient brightness is, however, essential because the birder frequently must deal with the poor light conditions of twilight, dense woodlands, and gray winter days. A good general rule to follow in judging the brightness of binoculars is to compare the magnification number with the number for the objective lens diameter; the lens diameter should be 5 times the magnification. Therefore, 7 × 35, 8 × 40, and 10 × 50 binoculars have objective lenses of sufficient size for their magnifying power.

Binoculars will range in price from fifty or sixty dollars a pair to around a thousand dollars. I recommend one of the following brands for birdwatching: Swift, Bausch & Lomb, Nikon, Bushnell, Leitz, or Zeiss. Leitz, Zeiss, and Bausch & Lomb make the most expensive binoculars; their quality is unsurpassed. Fortunately, there are many other excellent binoculars available within a reasonable price range. The other brands mentioned have optics that are priced from the low end of the scale upward. Nikon, for example, has an outstanding series of sports optics over a price range that can suit almost everybody. My personal favorite in birdwatching optics comes from Bushnell. For price and quality the Bushnell series is the best bargain. You get the advantage of high power, superb brightness and clarity, rugged construction, and long life, all for around two hundred dollars. Don't be afraid to spend money on a good pair of binoculars. They are an investment for a lifetime of enjoyment.

Attracting Birds

Entire books have been written about attracting birds to your yard, and I will not go into detail here except to offer a few general suggestions. Three things will attract birds: food, water, and shelter.

The easiest of these to provide is water, which birds need for drinking and bathing. It may be a shallow pan of water on an apartment balcony, a fancy birdbath out in the back yard, or even a landscaped pond dug into the ground. Regardless of how you choose to provide it, water is the most important gift you can give to urban birds, particularly in times of drought.

Sunflower seeds, cracked corn, millet, thistle, milo, hulled oats, and wheat are important foods for birds and they are commercially available. Place them in shallow pans or in special feeders (watch out for raids by squirrels). Other foods usable in feeders are fruits, nuts, and bread. Pine cones stuffed with peanut butter are a nice treat. Feeders will attract many of the common urban birds like jays, cardinals, grackles, starlings, chickadees, and titmice. Hummingbirds will be attracted to special hummingbird feeders that dispense sugary liquid.

And last, birds need shelter for roosting and nesting. You can buy or build housing, like bluebird houses and the ever-popular martin houses, or you can provide shelter with trees and shrubbery. Plants are also an important food source for birds if they produce edible seeds, fruit, or nectar.

Visit your local nursery and get suggestions for attracting bird life through landscaping. One of the best books on this subject is *The Audubon Society Guide To Attracting Birds* by Stephen W. Kress (Scribner, 1985). This comprehensive work covers all phases of attracting bird life by feeders, water systems, landscaping, and housing.

The birds of Houston are out there waiting for you in all their beauty and fascination. Go out and enjoy them!

Northern Mockingbird

Few birds are as well known or as beloved as the mockingbird, the state bird of Texas. The mockingbird is short on physical beauty but long on personality, and its crystalline singing is as natural to Texas as the armadillo or the prickly-pear cactus.

The mockingbird, formally known as the NORTHERN MOCKINGBIRD, is dull gray with off-white undersides, a long tail, and large white patches on the outer half of the wings. The tail has white outer feathers. In flight, the wing patches flash and, with the long tail and gray color, serve to identify the bird at a distance.

Common year round in Houston, the bird lives throughout the state in almost any kind of habitat, except in dense forests and in regions completely devoid of trees and shrubs. In the city, look for the mockingbird in parks and neighborhoods, along roadsides and woodland edges, on power lines and fences, and in trees and shrubs; you won't have to look very long.

The mockingbird often flies short distances in a gentle arc from tree to tree, feeding on berries or insects while twitching its tail, and quickly moving on.

It will sing throughout most of the year, and in the breeding season of spring and early summer the melodies of this sassy, conspicuous bird will grace the daylight hours and often late into the night. I recall once being awakened well after midnight in the spring by a boisterous songster in the back yard. High up in a large sycamore tree, in the clear bright moonlight, a mockingbird was cheerfully singing, oblivious to the late hour. The bird's repertoire will often be its own call notes interspersed with sounds of mimicry of other birds. The bluejay, with its harsh "jay, jay," seems to be a favorite object of imitation.

The mockingbird is not shy about showing its displeasure if intruders enter its nesting territory. This belligerent bird fears nothing; people, dogs, cats, squirrels, and other birds have at one time or another been in the sights of an angry, swooping mockingbird intent on protecting its nest and banishing the offender.

NORTHERN MOCKINGBIRD

Mimus polyglottos

Field Marks: 10 in., pale gray bird with lighter
underparts, moderately long tail with
white outer feathers, and large white wing
patches

Habitat: neighborhoods, parks, roadsides, open
areas with occasional trees or shrubbery

Occurrence: all year

Behavior: solitary, frequently sings, aggressive in
spring and early summer when nesting

1. Northern Mockingbird

Blue Jay

I once asked my good friend Ben Feltner to name his favorite bird. Ben is a professional birder who began birdwatching as a child in his native England and who has led birding tours throughout the United States, Latin America, Europe, and Australia. He has seen more birds than most of us know to exist, and his favorite bird is the BLUE JAY.

Intelligent, handsome, and full of personality, the blue jay is unmistakable in its dashing, military blue plumage. Its back and wings are blue; the wings have white spots and black stripes. The face and underparts are grayish-white, the head is crested, and a black necklace reaches across the upper chest.

The blue jay ranges throughout the city, and it can be found every month of the year, frequently calling with its screechy "jay! jay!" You'll usually see the blue jay in wooded neighborhoods, where it moves about tree limbs looking for insects and small fruits. The bird will sweep in quickly, move alertly about the branches, then fly off to the next stop. The blue jay is not a modest bird. When it is in your yard, you will know it. Either you will hear its raucous call, or you will see it perched in a tree in its brilliant plumage.

BLUE JAY

Cyanocitta cristata

Field Marks: 11–12 in., crested head, blue back, head,
and tail, face and underparts lighter, black
necklace, large white patches on wings
Habitat: neighborhoods, parks, yards
Occurrence: all year
Behavior: noisy, conspicuous, energetic

2. Blue Jay

Ring-billed Gull

The RING-BILLED GULL is the most commonly seen gull within the Houston area. These agile, buoyant fliers gather, often in large numbers, in parking lots and landfills, where they scavenge for edible refuse.

The ring-billed gull is larger than the laughing gull and smaller than the herring gull, two other species of gulls that are common on the coast but seldom seen within the city limits. The ring-billed is usually the only Texas gull that will be found inland in large numbers in the winter, especially around freshwater lakes and waterways.

In the adult plumage its head, upper back, chest, and belly are white. The back and wings are gray. Immature birds have dark streaking over the head, neck, and underparts. When the bird is in flight, the black wingtips marked with large white spots are a good field mark. The best field mark is the black band around the upper and lower halves of the yellow beak, very close to the tip; it looks like a strip of electrical tape. The legs are yellow.

Gulls are among the most graceful of birds, and often, long before you get close to them to see any identifying features, you can recognize them in flight. A few beats of their long, powerful wings will bring them high aloft with an elegant economy of effort, and in the air they capture the wind with ease and grace.

RING-BILLED GULL

Larus delawarensis

Field Marks: 18–20 in., white head, chest, and upper back, gray wings and back, black band around tip of yellow beak

Habitat: open areas where edible refuse is left, parking lots, landfills, inland lakes

Occurrence: September through May

Behavior: graceful flight, often in flocks

3. Ring-billed Gull

House Sparrow

If the rock dove is the reigning avian presence in the canyons of downtown, the HOUSE SPARROW reigns everywhere else. It pervades neighborhoods and parks and yards and just about any other open area in the city. The bird was introduced from its native England into New York City's Central Park in the 1850s, and it has spread to the cities and towns of the entire country. The environment of the city has been especially hospitable to the house sparrow; although the bird has been found in every county in Texas, it has flourished where there are houses and other buildings.

The house sparrow feeds on grain and seeds, as well as on insects and garden produce like fruits and berries, which are abundant in the urban environment. House sparrows are little, bouncy birds that hop around on the ground in small flocks while foraging. They will also be seen in trees and bushes, and they commonly nest in rain gutters on buildings.

Males and females differ in plumage, the male being the more attractive of the two. He has a gray crown, black throat and upper chest, large gray patches below the eye, and a chestnut nape and stripe through the eye. In both sexes the back is brown, streaked with black, and the underparts are dull gray. The female lacks any other distinctive markings except for a pale brown eyebrow.

HOUSE SPARROW

Passer domesticus

Field Marks: 6 in., mostly brown over back and lighter
                below; males have black throat, chestnut
                nape and eyestripe, and gray on side of
                face
Habitat: throughout city except deep woodlands
Occurrence: all year
Behavior: hops on ground in small flocks, noisy and
                active

4. House Sparrow (pair)
   At nest in purple martin house

DOVES

Four species of doves thrive in Houston: the rock dove (also known as the pigeon), the mourning dove, the Inca dove, and the ringed turtle-dove. Although they vary in size and color, they all have the body shape characteristic of this family of powerful fliers: a plump, chesty body with a small, rounded head that bobs back and forth while the bird walks.

Doves feed on the ground, where they strut about on their short legs, pecking for seeds and grain. Often they feed in small flocks along roadsides and railroad beds and in yards and parks. You will often see them perched on power lines. They are well adapted to the city.

The ROCK DOVE is the largest and most numerous of Houston-area doves, the familiar "pigeon" of the urban landscape. Is there any other bird that embodies the vitality of the big city more than the rock dove? What would Trafalgar Square or the Piazza San Marco be without it?

Today's urban pigeons are descendants of birds that were domesticated from the wild rock dove that was native to the Old World, where it nested and roosted on rocky cliffs. During the nineteenth century, domestic doves were bred from this wild type by bird breeders in England and elsewhere. As domestic birds were released to the wild over the years, they established the free-living population of city pigeons. The bird was eventually introduced into North America, where it readily adapted to buildings and bridges and other structures that served as substitutes for the cliffs of Europe.

Unlike most birds, the rock dove exhibits a wide range of color patterns, but it also has a "standard" plumage derived from its wild ancestor. This standard plumage is a light gray body with two dark wing stripes, a white rump, and a dark head and neck that are overlaid with a purple iridescence. The rock dove can appear all dark, mostly white, or any intermediate of reddish-brown or gray. Its call is a gurgling "oo-roo-coo" or "coo-roo-coo."

The MOURNING DOVE is a slender bird with a body of pastel pink-brown and darker brown wings. Other field marks are dark spots on the wings, orange legs, and a long tail. When the bird flies, the tail spreads into a lancet shape and shows white tips on the outer tail feathers. When the bird takes off, its wings make a soft whistling sound. In males the head and neck have a faint purple iridescence. The bird's call is a mournful "cooo-cooo-coo."

The INCA DOVE, the smallest member of this group of city doves, is the most "exotic." The dark edges of its light brown feathers give the bird its best field mark, a distinctive "scaly" appearance. In flight the Inca dove reveals two additional identifying characteristics, which are a long, squared-off tail with white outer feathers and a large, chestnut patch toward the end of each wing. Its call is "ooh-coo," each syllable equally stressed.

The RINGED TURTLE-DOVE is the least common of our urban doves; it will be seen in only a few locations throughout town. It first became established in Bellaire from escaped cage birds. This dove is a very pale bird, slightly smaller than the rock dove. The chest and neck are lighter than the pale brown back and wings. Its tail is long and narrow. A narrow black ring, the best field mark, goes around the back and sides of the neck; the ring does not join in front. The bird's call is "coo-hr-r-r-rooh."

5. *Rock Dove*
  Showing wide variation in plumage

ROCK DOVE

Columba livia

Field Marks:	12–13 in., much variation in plumage, basic type gray with two dark wing stripes, dark, glossy head and neck, white rump
Habitat:	city buildings, overpasses, roadsides
Occurrence:	all year
Behavior:	feeds on ground in flocks

MOURNING DOVE

Zenaida macroura

Field Marks:	11–13 in., pink-brown plumage on underparts, darker brown above, lancet-shaped tail shows white-tipped outer feathers in flight, whistling sound made on take-off, dark spots on wings
Habitat:	yards, parks, neighborhoods
Occurrence:	all year
Behavior:	feeds on ground in small flocks

6. *Mourning Dove*

7. *Inca Dove*

8. Ringed Turtle-Dove

INCA DOVE

Columbina inca

Field Marks:	7–8 in., long tail with white outer feathers, rufous patches in wings, scaly appearance
Habitat:	yards, parks, neighborhoods
Occurrence:	all year
Behavior:	feeds on ground in small flocks

RINGED TURTLE-DOVE

Streptopelia risoria

Field Marks:	11–13 in., pale plumage, lighter on underparts, incomplete black ring around back of neck, long tail
Habitat:	yards, neighborhoods, power lines
Occurrence:	infrequently seen, very localized, most often observed in Bellaire
Behavior:	usually solitary, perched or feeding on ground

WOODPECKERS

The woodpeckers are among the most immediately recognizable and most interesting of the city's birds. Already highly specialized for flight, these stout, perky birds have unique adaptations for feeding, perching, and nesting in trees.

A woodpecker's head and neck are specially cushioned to protect the brain and spinal cord from the thousands of blows a day that these delicate organs receive. The heavy beak allows chiseling and digging in tree bark, and a special bony apparatus at the back of the mouth pushes the tongue out well past the tip of the beak to search out insects hidden under the bark. The short, stout legs have long, clawed toes that permit agile climbing. Finally, the short, stiff wedge-shaped tail, when pressed against a tree trunk, provides stability and leverage while the bird is pecking and foraging.

From the birder's point of view, woodpeckers can be difficult to watch and enjoy. I have found them to be generally evasive and intolerant of anyone approaching too close. When they sense an observer, they move behind the trunk or just fly away. When you see a woodpecker, approach it gently. A woodpecker endows a tree with a special, if fleeting, beauty.

Six species of woodpeckers occur regularly within wooded areas of the city: the pileated, red-headed, red-bellied, and downy woodpeckers, the common flicker, and the yellow-bellied sapsucker. (Yes, there really is such a bird.) The downy, pileated, and red-bellied reside in the city year round.

These energetic birds move about constantly, walking up and down trunks and climbing out on limbs (except for the ground-feeding flicker), pecking and digging and whacking away at the bark. A woody staccato signals a woodpecker's presence, and it is an inviting sound.

One of the most abundant and commonly seen birds of this group is the RED-BELLIED WOODPECKER. A word of caution: don't rely on seeing the red belly. It is very faint and not necessary for identification. Look for the horizontal black-and-white barring on the back and the pale belly, chest, face, and throat. Males have a bright red crown and nape; in females the red stops at the back of the head, with the crown and forehead pale.

By far the most impressive of the local woodpeckers is the PILEATED WOODPECKER, the largest of North America's twenty-two woodpecker species. This nearly all-black woodpecker has a brilliant red crest, a black moustache, and a broad white stripe that extends along the face and down the neck. The wings display large white patches when the bird is in flight. In males the red extends over the forehead; females have the red crest, but the forehead and forecrown are black.

With its small size and lack of bold coloration, the little DOWNY WOODPECKER, although common throughout the city, is the least noticeable of Houston's woodpeckers. The downy is completely white on the underparts. The wings are black with horizontal white barring. The back is white, and from a distance it appears as a broad white vertical stripe between the dark wings. This vertical white stripe is the downy's key field mark, along with its smallness. The face is marked with horizontal black and white stripes. A close look at a male will reveal a small patch of red on the crown, although this frequently is not evident.

Beginning in October, the YELLOW-BELLIED SAPSUCKER moves into the southern states from its northern range, to remain there until early May. Slightly larger than the downy, the sapsucker is best identified by a white wing patch that appears as a vertical stripe along the bird's side when it is perched. Other useful field marks are the red forehead and crown, the back mottled with black and white, and a black-and-white striped facial pattern. The throat is red on the male, white on the female. Both sexes have a black upper chest and a pale yellow belly.

"Sapsucker holes" are a horizontal row of holes that the bird drills in a tree trunk to feed on the sap and the insects attracted by it; they decorate many trees in the city.

The RED-HEADED WOODPECKER is the most boldly colored of the native woodpeckers, the easiest to identify, and the dressiest of all. Unfortunately, it is the least observed within the city, except for specific locations.

The head, neck, and throat are a solid, brilliant red that would be the envy of a Roman prelate. The back and most of the bird's wings are black. The chest, belly, and rump are bright white. The inner rear edges of the wing are also white; when the bird is perched these wing feathers appear as a triangular white patch over the lower back. The red-headed woodpecker is most often observed in Houston from April to October.

The NORTHERN FLICKER departs from the standard woodpecker color scheme of red, black, and white. And also unlike other woodpeckers, the flicker feeds on the ground, where it searches for ants, its main food.

The flicker is a large bird with black and brown horizontal striping over the back, a broad black patch on the upper chest, large black spots over lighter underparts, and a white rump patch that is seen in the flying bird. The face

9. *Red-bellied Woodpecker (male)*
   Shows typical barbed tongue of woodpeckers

is brown, and the crown and nape are gray. The back of
the head has a bright red spot. Males have a bold black
moustache.

RED-BELLIED

WOODPECKER

Melanerpes carolinus

Field Marks:	8–9 in., red crown (male) and nape, pale gray face and underparts, black-and-white horizontal barring over back
Habitat:	trees in parks and neighborhoods
Occurrence:	all year
Behavior:	forages in trees over trunks and branches

PILEATED WOODPECKER

Dryocopus pileatus

Field Marks: 16–19 in., mostly black, white stripes
along neck and face, red crest
Habitat: trees in parks and neighborhoods
Occurrence: all year
Behavior: pecks vigorously and loudly on trunks, in
flight resembles crow

DOWNY WOODPECKER

Picoides pubescens

Field Marks: 6 in., all-white underparts, vertical white
stripe down middle of back, short beak,
black-and-white striped facial pattern
Habitat: trees in yards and neighborhoods
Occurrence: all year
Behavior: common but often inconspicuous

10. *Pileated Woodpecker (male)*
    Feeding young at nest

11. Downy Woodpecker

12. Yellow-bellied Sapsucker (male)

YELLOW-BELLIED

SAPSUCKER

Sphyrapicus varius

Field Marks:	7–8 in., mottled black-and-white back, vertical white stripe down side of body, red forehead, black-and-white striped facial pattern, pale yellow belly
Habitat:	trees in parks and neighborhoods
Occurrence:	October through April
Behavior:	drills row of "sapsucker holes" in tree trunks

13. Yellow-bellied Sapsucker (female)

RED-HEADED

WOODPECKER

Melanerpes erythrocephalus

Field Marks: 7–8 in., brilliant red head and neck, white underparts, black back with white wing patch

Habitat: trees in parks and neighborhoods

Occurrence: April through October

Behavior: active through trees, forages on trunks and branches, tends to be localized

14. Red-headed Woodpecker

NORTHERN FLICKER

Colaptes auratus

Field Marks: 11–13 in., brownish overall, black and brown barring across back, heavy black spotting on underparts, tan face, gray crown with red spot on nape, moustache in males

Habitat: yards, semi-open woodlands

Occurrence: October through March

Behavior: feeds on ground for ants

15. Northern Flicker (female)

BLACKBIRDS

The "blackbirds" are a group of darkly colored birds that gather in large, conspicuous flocks throughout the city. They are gregarious and often raucous, and you won't have to travel far in town before you'll encounter at least one species. In Houston the most commonly observed blackbirds are the common grackle, the great-tailed grackle, the brown-headed cowbird, the red-winged blackbird, and two birds that are not true members of the blackbird family but that are included here because of their dark, shiny plumage—the American crow and the European starling.

At a distance the blackbirds look very similar; all are dark, all seem devoid of apparent color, and several are alike in shape. Each species, however, has one or more distinctive features that will become obvious to you with practice. To identify the blackbirds, first get a clear picture of the bird's size and the profile of its body and beak. Then, look for subtle, often beautiful coloration that will confirm identification.

At a length of a foot and a half or more, the AMERICAN CROW is the largest of our urban blackbirds. Hefty, black as obsidian, and sporting a large, heavy beak, the crow is one of the most familiar birds of the American landscape. It lives in lightly wooded areas throughout the city, such as parks and neighborhoods, and it often feeds along roadsides and open grassy areas. The crow consumes insects, grains, small reptiles and mammals, carrion, and edible garbage.

The crow flies on slow, steady beats of its strong, broad wings, and displays in flight a squared-off tail and a spreading of the feathers of the wingtips. Males and females are identical. And who among us would not recognize the crow's signature call, the loud, ragged-edged "caw! caw!"?

Grackles are noisy, sociable blackbirds that inhabit residential areas, parks, and other open spaces; they generally avoid the interior of heavily wooded areas. They are smaller and slimmer than the crow (although the great-tailed can be as long), and they have long, slender beaks. The two species found in the city, the great-tailed grackle and the common grackle, generally form individual flocks; the two species usually don't mingle.

A huge, keel-shaped tail identifies the male GREAT-TAILED GRACKLE. Looking somewhat like a sailboat hull, the tail is almost as long as the bird's body. The male also has a yellow eye and black plumage that shows a deep purple sheen on the head, neck, and back and blue on the breast. These colors show up best in bright sunlight. Females, often in company with males, are slightly smaller, with shorter tails and olive-brown plumage. The back is darker brown than the underparts.

Of all the blackbirds, the great-tailed grackle is the most interesting to watch. In spring during courtship several males strut around a bored-looking female, pointing their beaks skyward, holding their wings out, and ruffling their feathers. The female continues to peck about the ground, seemingly indifferent to this avian flirtation. The ritual appears to work, however; the birds are abundant.

When great-taileds gather in trees, they often make loud, screechy sounds that resemble someone rattling Venetian blinds.

The COMMON GRACKLE is a smaller version of the

great-tailed. This bird is shorter overall by a third than the larger species, and its tail, although still long, is proportionately shorter in relation to the body. The shiny black plumage is underlaid with a purple, green, and blue iridescence. The beak is slender and pointed; the eye is yellow. Females are duller and slightly smaller than males. Juveniles are dull brown.

Common grackles assemble in flocks in open areas, such as yards and parks and parking lots. Both species of grackles, like the crow, feed on a wide variety of insects, grain, and small animals.

The EUROPEAN STARLING was introduced into the United States in 1890 when sixty of the birds were released into Central Park in New York City. From this little group of avian immigrants the starling has multiplied across the land to a population of millions.

A stocky, upright bird, it is frequently seen feeding, like the grackles, in open, grassy areas throughout the city. But unlike the other blackbirds, the starling dresses, in its breeding plumage, in a speckled iridescence of purple and green over its entire body. The upperparts show a deeper tinge of purple, while the face, underparts, and wings have an underlying tinge of green. In this nuptial plumage the starling also shows one of its best field marks, a long, thin yellow beak. No other blackbird in the United States has a yellow beak. In winter the plumage becomes dull black spotted with white and the beak turns dark. The tail is short and squared-off.

If there was ever a bird that birdwatchers love to hate, it is the BROWN-HEADED COWBIRD. You may hate the brown-headed cowbird; it is encouraged that you do so. Why this strange recommendation? This abundant little pest is a brood parasite, a bandit of the nest. The cowbird lays its eggs in the nest of another species of bird, such as a wren or warbler, inducing the parent bird to raise the cowbird young instead of its own. Every cowbird you see is a songbird, a "good" bird, that could have been.

And on top of its parental impudence, the cowbird is woefully unattractive. It is short and stumpy, with a heavy wedgelike beak. The male has a dull brown head and dull black body; the female is gray-brown overall. The bird usually occurs in large flocks in open, grassy areas, although individuals will frequent parks and neighborhoods and power lines.

The RED-WINGED BLACKBIRD is perhaps the least common blackbird deep within the city. But as urban development gives way to fields, pastures, and agricultural areas on the city's outskirts, you will see this handsome, vivacious bird in Napoleonic plumage, often in huge flocks.

The male red-winged blackbird is black overall except for the bright red epaulets, or shoulder patches, visible on the upper part of the wing when the bird is at rest. A thin yellow trim lies along the bottom of the red patch, although you usually cannot see it at a distance.

The female is dark brown above and heavily streaked in brown over her underparts. Once in my early birding days when I saw a solitary female red-winged, I just knew I had come across some exotic warbler or other rarity. When she rejoined her better-marked male companion, my disappointment was keen, but I knew I had been taught something about field ornithology.

The blackbirds (except for the crow) are a highly gregarious group, well adapted to urban life. In the mornings you'll see waves of blackbirds heading out for the day's feeding; in the evening they will return to roost in trees. The flocks are usually grackles, but they can sometimes include cowbirds or red-wingeds. Densely wooded areas located throughout the city concentrate the birds for their evening rest, but the reason that flocks change places after a time is not fully understood. Roosting blackbirds, furthermore, can be a nuisance. The campus at Rice University, with its majestic live oaks, was a well-known roosting spot for many years. The campus administration had undertaken heroic efforts to scare the birds off, usually with little success. By the time I arrived on campus for graduate study in the early 1980s, the blackbirds had moved elsewhere. The birds at one time liked City Hall as well. I parked by the reflection pool one evening to attend a function downtown. By the time I returned, the blackbirds had moved into the oaks surrounding the pool. I had to find a late-night car wash.

AMERICAN CROW

Corvus brachyrhynchos

Field Marks: 17–18 in., all-black plumage, heavy beak,
                wingtip feathers spread in flight
Habitat: woodland edges, roadsides, parks
Occurrence: all year
Behavior: calls with the familiar "caw! caw!"

16. American Crow

GREAT-TAILED GRACKLE

Quiscalus mexicanus

Field Marks: male is large (18 in.) with very long, keel-shaped tail, black plumage with purple sheen on head, neck, and back; female is smaller (15 in.), dull brown overall
Habitat: open grassy areas, parking lots, trees
Occurrence: all year
Behavior: often in large flocks, noisy, conspicuous spring courtship

17. Great-tailed Grackle (male)

18. Great-tailed Grackle (female)

COMMON GRACKLE

Quiscalus quiscula

Field Marks: 12 1/2 in., smaller than great-tailed; male
              glossy black with purple iridescence on
              head, neck, and chest; female smaller and
              duller
Habitat: open grassy areas, parks, suburbs
Occurrence: all year
Behavior: noisy, gregarious, usually in flocks

19. Common Grackle

EUROPEAN STARLING

Sturnus vulgaris

Field Marks:	8 in., spring plumage marked by a complex streaking of purple and green iridescence; fall plumage brown with heavy white spotting on chest; beak is yellow in spring, dark the rest of the year
Habitat:	neighborhoods, open grassy areas, power lines, parks
Occurrence:	all year
Behavior:	often in flocks with grackles, feeds on ground like other blackbirds

20. European Starling

BROWN-HEADED

COWBIRD

Molothrus ater

Field Marks: 6–8 in., stumpy bird with stubby beak;
male has black body with dull brown
head; female is gray-brown overall

Habitat: open grassy areas, yards, neighborhoods,
parks

Occurrence: all year

Behavior: often in huge flocks, robs other species of
their young by brood parasitism

21. Brown-headed Cowbird (male)

22. Brown-headed Cowbird (female)

RED-WINGED BLACKBIRD

Agelaius phoeniceus

Field Marks:	9 in., male black with bright red shoulder patch; female heavily streaked brown
Habitat:	fields, pastures, agricultural areas at city's edge
Occurrence:	all year
Behavior:	often in enormous flocks, females keep to themselves in winter, high-pitched lilting "konk-la-ree" often heard throughout countryside

23. *Red-winged Blackbird (male)*

24. *Red-winged Blackbird (female)*

Northern Cardinal

Who among us does not instantly recognize the NORTHERN CARDINAL, or "redbird"? Resplendent in brilliant red and full of song and personality, the cardinal is one of the brightest and liveliest of our urban birds. Cardinals make their presence known as much by their song as by their colorful plumage. They are active, perky birds, sailing through woodlands, perching in trees, and frequently singing loudly with their repetitive, high-pitched "what-cheer, what-cheer." I have often heard the cardinal go on and on with its robust serenade almost to the point of annoyance.

The male is bright red on the crest, chest, and under-parts; the back is reddish-brown. The short, heavy beak is red-orange, and a black face patch surrounds its base. The cardinal is the only all-red crested bird found in this country.

The female is dull reddish-brown over the tail and wings and is buff-brown or buffy-olive over the back and under-parts. Her beak is orange, and the facial patch surround-ing it at the base is dark, but not the solid black of the male. Both sexes have a fairly long tail and an erectile crest, which gives the cardinal an alert, upright look. They often travel in pairs around residential areas, offering the observer a good opportunity to compare them.

In urban areas the cardinal dwells in forested or semi-open areas, such as wooded neighborhoods, parks, ar-boretums, and patches of woodland or shrubbery around the city. It moves about by short flights from perch to perch.

25. Northern Cardinal (male)

The bird eats seeds, grain, insects, and wild fruit; it frequently feeds at backyard bird feeders. The cardinal's heavy, conical beak attests to its diet of hard seeds and insects.

Cardinalis cardinalis

Field Marks: 7–9 in., male bright red; female dull red-brown; both sexes have prominent crest, black face, and a heavy, orange, conical beak

Habitat: wooded or semi-wooded areas, neighborhoods, parks

Occurrence: all year

Behavior: male and female often travel in pairs, loud, repetitive song note

26. *Northern Cardinal (female)*

BIRDS OF THE
SUMMER SKY

Each summer the sky over Houston becomes home to three species of birds which live a life more devoted to flight than any other bird you will see in the city. The purple martin, the chimney swift, and the common nighthawk move into the area in the spring, stay through the summer, and depart in the fall. They feed only on high-flying insects, catching them in their gaping mouths. In pursuit of food they spend almost all of their waking hours on the wing.

You will see these birds most often in flight and usually only at a distance. You can get a close look at them if they perch on a power line, but this is rare. Learn to identify the birds of the summer sky by three characteristics: the silhouette, the height in the air at which each bird usually flies, and the individual styles of flight.

The PURPLE MARTIN is one of the most popular urban birds because of the widespread belief that martins help control the mosquito population. You'll see martin houses—the boxes with entrance holes in them set high up on a pole—all over town. The martin belongs to the swallow family, and at eight inches in length, it is the largest North American member of this group of streamlined, acrobatic birds.

The male purple martin is deep, glossy purple-black overall; the female is duller with a gray chest. In flight the martin shows short, triangular-shaped wings and a long, forked tail. The martin is a vigorous flier; it flaps for short distances, glides briefly, then flaps again as it darts, dives, and wheels through the air.

The CHIMNEY SWIFT is the smallest and most energetic of the three species. This dark brown bird is often described as a "cigar with wings." Its stubby, cigar-shaped body is borne aloft by long, narrow wings that form a gentle arc when extended. Unlike the martin and the nighthawk, both of whom occasionally perch, the chimney swift is never observed except in flight. The swift flies intensely, often in small flocks, darting about with rapid wingbeats and frequently emitting a high-pitched chatter.

In the evenings chimney swifts form a giant, living funnel as they spiral down into an inactive chimney to roost for the night. Years ago I lived in an apartment complex in Bellaire that overlooked an old, abandoned incinerator. Each evening I would watch the swifts as they swirled far above the top of the chimney and then descended into it in a rapid, ever-tightening gyre.

Of all the birds of the summer sky, I love the COMMON NIGHTHAWK the most. This gentle bird flies the highest of all, often to where you can barely see it. The nighthawk has long, narrow, pointed wings—much longer in proportion to the body than the martin's or the swift's—and flies with deep wingbeats in a slow, jerky pattern.

The nighthawk's plumage is mottled blackish-brown; the wings have broad white bands across the outer half. The tail is long and slightly forked. Frequently you will hear the nighthawk's high-pitched, nasal "peent" drifting down from high above before you see the bird. Despite their name, nighthawks fly during the day as well as at night.

Purple martins first arrive in the city from their winter range in the tropics in late January or early February, when "scouts" come looking for homesites. They stay through the summer and depart by September. The chimney swift is most commonly seen from late March to mid-October; the common nighthawk from late April to mid-October.

Although the heights at which these birds fly overlap, in general the chimney swift will be observed closest to the ground, the purple martin higher up (just above the rooftops of houses), and the nighthawk will often fly well up into the air. The martin and the swift can also fly high, but because of their smaller size, they are not so easily seen as the larger nighthawk.

The birds of the summer sky have always given me a sense of hope. They flourish amid the concrete and steel and bustle of the great city, and they animate the sky with their grace and energy. It is somehow a deep comfort to me that I can walk out of the Alley Theater late on a summer evening and hear the high, buzzy cry of the nighthawk echoing among the skyscrapers.

PURPLE MARTIN

Progne subis

Field marks: 7–8 in., male deep, glossy purple-black;
               female duller with gray underparts; short
               broad-based wings, long forked tail
Habitat: the sky during the day, martin houses at
               night and during day
Occurrence: March through August
Behavior: flies by alternating wingbeats with gliding

27. *Purple Martin (male)*

28. *Purple Martin (female)*

CHIMNEY SWIFT

Chaetura pelagica

Field Marks: 5–6 in., both sexes dull dark brown; long, narrow wings held back in arc, cigar-shaped body

Habitat: in the air constantly during daylight hours, roosts in chimneys at night

Occurrence: late March through mid-October

Behavior: intensely energetic flight, frequently emits a high-pitched chatter, often gathers in small flocks

29. *Chimney Swift*
Rehabilitated bird in hand;
note stiff tail and long wings

COMMON NIGHTHAWK

Chordeiles minor

Field Marks:	8–10 in., darkly mottled brown plumage; long, narrow wings with broad white band near tip of each
Habitat:	the sky, frequently at great heights; sometimes perches on power lines during the day
Occurrence:	late April through mid-October
Behavior:	active by day and night, usually solitary, flies with slow wingbeats and jerky flight path

30. Common Nighthawk (male)

Cedar Waxwing

The CEDAR WAXWING is one of the bird-watching joys of the Houston winter. Beginning in late November, this sleek, racy bird moves into the city, dashing about in tight, quick flocks, feeding on pyracantha and other berry-producing shrubbery.

The bird is a flying confection. Its head, neck, and upperparts are butterscotch brown. The short squared-off tail has a lemon-yellow band across the tip, and bright cherry-red waxy-looking spots dot the tips of the secondary flight feathers, giving the bird its name. The waxwing's crested head sports its signature broad black eyemask. The plumage always looks silky smooth and unruffled.

Although waxwings can be sighted as solitary individuals, they most often move throughout the city in tight, rapidly flying flocks that seem to function as a single organism. A golden-brown cloud of these perky, energetic birds will descend on a tree or bush, feed actively for a few minutes, then in unison take off for the next destination.

Waxwings will occasionally eat insects, but berries and fruit from trees and shrubs are the mainstays of their diet. Among their favorites are mulberry, pyracantha, loquat, and the cedar. The bird, therefore, forages within the city around areas marked by ornamental and native fruit-bearing vegetation, like neighborhoods, parks, and woodland edges.

CEDAR WAXWING

Bombycilla cedrorum

Field Marks:	7–8 in., smooth light brown plumage, yellow band across tip of tail, red spots on secondaries, crested head with bold black eyemask
Habitat:	parks, neighborhoods, lightly wooded areas, usually observed in trees or shrubs
Occurrence:	late November to early May
Behavior:	gregarious, usually moves about in dense, active flocks.

31. Cedar Waxwing

Killdeer

The KILLDEER is the urban cousin of the plovers, a group of perky, upright birds that live along the world's coastlines. This attractive shorebird can be found not only on sandy shores and coastal prairies but also in parking lots, city parks, and numerous other open areas throughout the state.

The killdeer has a white underside, a brown back, and two bold black bands across the breast. In flight the bird displays an orange-brown rump and a white stripe down the length of each wing. The upright profile of the killdeer is characteristic of the plovers.

The killdeer always seems to be in a hurry. It struts quickly about the ground on long, flesh-colored legs, vigilant while pecking for bugs, seeds, and worms. Then, at seemingly the slightest provocation, it darts away over the ground in a low, swift flight, only to land soon and continue its alert and vigorous foraging.

Among the North American plovers, the killdeer is the most widely distributed. It is found throughout the city and the state and, indeed, throughout all of the United States and most of Canada and Mexico. Nearly any kind of open or semi-open habitat will support a population of the gregarious killdeer; the bird does not inhabit dense woodlands.

When you encounter a killdeer sitting on its shallow scrape of a nest on the ground (usually in less-developed areas), you are likely to be treated to the "broken-wing" display, for which the bird is famous. To distract an intruder from the nest, the bird gyrates around with its wings spread out on the ground.

The killdeer cries with a sweet, plaintive whistle—a high-pitched, clear "deeee, deeee"; the call note is, in fact, the inspiration for the name "killdeer," and it is a joyful note of natural music heard amid the sounds of the city.

KILLDEER

Charadrius vociferus

Field Marks:	9–11 in., brown back, white underparts, two black bands across breast, upright plover posture, orange-brown rump seen in flight, longitudinal white stripe on each wing
Habitat:	parks, fields, pastures
Occurrence:	all year
Behavior:	often in small groups, "broken wing" display, high-pitched, plaintive whistle

32. Killdeer
  On nest

Northern Harrier

The harriers are a group of hawks, widespread throughout Europe, that are represented in North America by only one species, the NORTHERN HARRIER. Formerly known as the marsh hawk, this bird of prey flies over large fields and pastures just outside the city and beyond; it doesn't occur deep within the city.

You will most often see this handsome, common raptor as it hunts rabbits and rodents by flying low over the ground in a leisurely, jerky flight pattern. The bird gently rocks side to side with its long, narrow wings slightly angled over the back. It veers one way, then another, and yet another as it covers ground like a reconnaissance plane scouting enemy territory.

The trim harrier lacks the heft of the great buteos (the large hawks) of the Houston area, the red-tailed and red-shouldered hawks. Its head is relatively small and rounded, the body slender, and the tail long and narrow. At the base of the tail is a large white patch that serves as the best identifying mark for this bird of prey.

Female harriers are brown over the back, and the undersides are lighter with heavy brown streaking. Males are pale steely gray over the back, and lighter below. Immature birds, which are numerous, closely resemble adult females. In the field, therefore, the great majority of birds observed have brown plumage. You will see adult males much less often. Occasionally you'll see a northern harrier perched on a fence post or on the ground, but mostly you will see them from the highway in their low, leisurely flight over marshes and fields.

NORTHERN HARRIER

Circus cyaneus

Field Marks: 16–24 in., slender build, small rounded head, long narrow wings, long narrow tail with large white patch at base, bird often visible from a distance; females and immatures brown; males pale gray-blue

Habitat: open fields, pastures, marshes

Occurrence: September through April

Behavior: usually solitary; low, erratic flight over open areas

33. Northern Harrier

HAWKS

Two species of buteo hawks commonly occur within the city, the red-tailed hawk and the red-shouldered hawk. The buteos are a group of large-bodied hawks that are smaller than the eagles but larger than other raptors, such as the accipiter hawks (a group of smaller, slender hawks like the Cooper's and sharp-shinned), the kestrel, and the Mississippi kite.

The RED-TAILED HAWK, more so than perhaps any other bird in its family, displays a wide and confusing variation in plumage, and this has been the nemesis of many a beginning hawk-watcher. Learning a few consistent field marks, however, will allow you to recognize this majestic bird of prey almost every time you encounter it.

The standard plumage of the red-tailed hawk is a dark brown back and upperparts, a rusty-red tail, a broad band of vertical dark streaks across the central portion of the otherwise light chest, and a dark patch along the inner leading edge of the underwing. No two red-taileds seem to look exactly alike. Immature birds, melanistic (very dark) specimens, various subspecies, and hybrids between different subspecies will show great variation in this typical plumage. Immature birds, for example, lack the classic red tail. But nearly all of them will show several predictable features.

If you view the bird from the rear when it is at rest (for example, perched on a utility pole), the red-tailed hawk displays a large, white, somewhat ragged V over its back. The V is not always immediately distinct but generally becomes apparent with close observation. Also, when the hawk is at rest as well as in flight the namesake rich, reddish-brown tail is an excellent field mark. When viewed from the front, most red-tailed hawks show a central band of dark vertical streaking across the light underparts.

At first glance, the RED-SHOULDERED HAWK is extremely similar to the slightly larger red-tailed hawk, but a good look at both will reveal several important differences. First, the underparts of the red-shouldered are much darker than the typical red-tailed's, since it is completely marked with reddish-brown horizontal barring. Second, the tail of the red-shouldered hawk is distinctly marked with several light bands, while lacking the smooth, strong rusty-red color of the red-tailed. Third, the red-shouldered hawk has a deep rusty-red shoulder patch near the top of each wing when the bird is at rest. The patch is usually distinct from the duller brown of the surrounding plumage of the wing and back. In flight, the red-shouldered hawk shows a translucent white crescent, or "window," toward the tip of the underside of each wing.

The two hawks usually live in different habitats. The red-shouldered hawk prefers more heavily wooded areas, while the red-tailed hawk prefers wide-open vistas like fields and pastures with few trees. Both birds are excellent hunters with extraordinarily keen eyesight with which they watch for rabbits, rodents, and other small animal life.

From October through April red-tailed hawks become numerous around Houston as birds from the northern parts of their range move south to avoid the harsh northern winter. During the summer months the numbers of red-tailed hawks greatly decline as they migrate back to the North.

The relatively common red-shouldered hawk is found in the city throughout the year, but in general the red-tailed hawk will be seen much more often than its less-conspicuous counterpart. It is recommended that any hawk sighted in the Houston area, especially in winter, should be considered a red-tailed hawk until proven otherwise.

34. Red-tailed Hawk

RED-TAILED HAWK

Buteo jamaicensis

Field Marks: 19–25 in., robust, brown over back with lighter, partially streaked chest, rusty-red tail, ragged white V over back, inner portion of leading edge of underwing black where wing adjoins body (note: this description fits only the standard adult plumage, not subspecies or immatures)

Habitat: open fields and pastures

Occurrence: October through April

Behavior: usually observed perched in tree or on utility pole at edge of open area, often seen soaring

RED-SHOULDERED HAWK

Buteo lineatus

Field Marks: 17–24 in., large hawk (smaller than red-tailed), in standard adult plumage dark brown over back, reddish-brown barring over chest, barred tail, rusty-red shoulder patch, white "window" near wingtip observed in flight

Habitat: wooded areas, river bottoms, neighborhoods

Occurrence: all year

Behavior: usually observed in flight or perched in tree

35. Red-shouldered Hawk

American Kestrel

The AMERICAN KESTREL, although it was formerly called the sparrow hawk, belongs to the falcon family. Measuring only eight to ten inches in length for the males (females are slightly larger), it is the smallest North American member of this exciting family of birds of prey.

The kestrel is a compact, powerful, and boldly patterned raptor that hunts by hovering over open fields and pastures in search of mice, small birds, and large insects. The kestrel's hovering flight, whereby it stays briefly in place in midair by the rapid beating of its long, pointed wings, is often an excellent aid in identifying the bird.

A male kestrel has blue-gray wings and a buff-brown nape and back; the upper chest is also buff brown and the white belly is dotted with large black spots. The crown of his rounded head is blue-gray, and the cheeks are white with large black patches at the rear edge of the white area. The tail is reddish-brown; the back and wings are also dotted with black spots. A vertical moustache stripe lies at the base of the beak.

The female lacks the steely blue coloration of the male. She is reddish-brown with black barring over the back and wings. The light brown underparts are streaked with darker brown. The female's head is similar to the male's, but the colors are less intense and her crown is brown instead of blue-gray.

When not in flight, kestrels can often be observed on a power line. The bird is rarely seen in Houston in summer, but it becomes numerous in the area from September to early April.

AMERICAN KESTREL

Falco sparverius

Field Marks: 8–11 in., bold facial pattern, small size,
                rounded head; blue and tan pattern in
                male; reddish-brown pattern in female
Habitat: open areas, fields, pastures
Occurrence: September through early April
Behavior: powerful, hovering flight

36. *American Kestrel (male)*

Eastern Meadowlark

Driving in the countryside can be boring, but a sure way to lift your spirits is to listen for the sweet, silvery whistle of the meadowlark. Its joyful song pervades the country air, like the scent of spring grass.

The EASTERN MEADOWLARK is a stout bird of the open country, but it is also found within the city in large, grassy fields and pastures. Viewed from the rear, the meadowlark blends well with its surroundings because of the streaky, dull brown plumage over its back. The bird's underparts, visible from the front, make no attempt at camouflage. A brilliant lemon-yellow breast and belly are marked with a large black V at the bottom of the throat. The throat above the V is also yellow. The bill is long and pointed, the crown is striped, and the tail is short.

The bird flies intensely for brief distances, spreading its short tail to display white outer tail feathers. It will also forage along the roadside, often in small flocks, as well as fly around a field or pasture in search of insects in warm weather and seeds and grain in winter.

The meadowlark's song is a series of five or six high-pitched, clear notes that descend in pitch toward the end.

The western meadowlark is also found in the Houston area, but sightings are rare. Although it is virtually identical to the eastern meadowlark, experienced observers can distinguish the two, usually by differences in song.

EASTERN MEADOWLARK

Sturnella magna

Field Marks: 7–10 in., streaky brown back, bright yellow breast and throat with black V, white outer tail feathers visible in flight
Habitat: fields, pastures, open grassy areas
Occurrence: all year
Behavior: intense flight close to ground, clear melodious series of song notes, often gathers in small flocks

37. Eastern Meadowlark

Mississippi Kite

The kites are a group of slender, agile birds of prey that soar and glide on long, pointed wings. Of the five species of United States kites, three occur in southeast Texas, and one of them, the MISSISSIPPI KITE, is a conspicuous late summer migrant through Houston. (The other two local species, the swallow-tailed kite and the black-shouldered kite, are seldom seen in the city.)

Most of the time you will see the Mississippi kite as it slowly flies low and easy over rooftops and trees in search of flying insects. It doesn't move at the breakneck pace of the chimney swift, or even as quickly as the purple martin; a much larger bird than those two species, the kite takes life a bit easier by gliding on outstretched wings, although it can put on a burst of speed when necessary.

On the infrequent occasions when you see a Mississippi kite perched, you can observe its dark gray body and wings, rounded, pale grey head, and strong, hooked beak. Seen from below in flight, the kite's silhouette is the best key to identification: a large, dark bird with long, pointed wings and a long, squared-off black tail, gliding smoothly in search of prey. The undersides of the wings are darker toward the tips and the rear edges.

Immature birds are sighted frequently. They are marked by a streaked breast and barred tail, in contrast to the evenly colored body and tail of the adult.

Kites come through the Houston area in scant numbers beginning in March, but they are commonly observed in August through early September.

MISSISSIPPI KITE

Ictinia mississippiensis

Field Marks:	14 in., dark gray body, long, pointed dark wings, long black squared-off tail, pale rounded head with hooked beak
Habitat:	open sky, occasionally seen perched in tall trees
Occurrence:	rare in spring and early summer, most common in August through early September
Behavior:	graceful gliding flight over tops of trees and houses

38. Mississippi Kite

Loggerhead Shrike

Loggerhead shrikes are a paradox. They belong to the songbirds, a large and diverse group generally associated with innocent twittering in the trees, but to a lizard or mouse or grasshopper they are a rapid and certain death racing from the sky. The LOGGERHEAD SHRIKE is also called the "butcher bird," since it makes no secret of its predatory way of life. Often when it kills, it will impale the prey on a cactus thorn or on a fence barb. The bird will then return later to eat.

The shrike is gray over the back, nape, and crown and gray-white below, and it has a short hooked bill and a bold black eyemask that suggests, appropriately enough, a masked bandit. The bird frequently flies from perch to perch in a low sweeping arc, displaying black wings with a white patch toward the tip.

Its flight characteristics and striped wings may lead the observer to think it is a mockingbird, but the shrike is darker, smaller, and more boldly patterned over the head. With practice you will be able to recognize immediately this common bird at a distance from its profile, flight pattern, and distinctive black, gray, and white plumage.

The shrike usually perches on power lines or on the outer reaches of tree canopies overlooking fields and pastures, from which it can survey the ground for small animal life. Once when I was walking through a pasture I came across a large lubber grasshopper stuck on a rusty fence barb. I knew the loggerhead shrike had been there before me.

LOGGERHEAD SHRIKE

Lanius ludovicianus

Field Marks: 8–10 in., gray above, gray-white below,
              black wings with white patches, short
              hooked bill, bold black eyemask
Habitat: open areas, fields, pastures
Occurrence: all year
Behavior: often perched on power lines, low
              sweeping flight from perch to perch,
              impales prey on sharp objects

39. Loggerhead Shrike

BIRDS OF THE
WOODLANDS

At various times of the year the Houston birdwatcher will encounter one or more of a group of small, perky birds that forage in woodlands. Because of their quick, flitty movements, small size, and tendency to forage, often in poor light, high in the dense foliage of trees, these common birds often present a serious challenge to the novice observer.

The birds are the Carolina wren, Carolina chickadee, tufted titmouse, ruby-crowned kinglet, orange-crowned warbler, yellow-rumped warbler, and blue-gray gnatcatcher. They inhabit either dense stands of woods or open or semi-open areas of mature trees, as found in heavily wooded parks and neighborhoods. Except for the wren, which more often forages in thick shrubbery and undergrowth, these energetic, acrobatic birds generally will be seen making their way over the limbs and branches of trees, often high up, searching for small insects.

The CAROLINA WREN is the largest bird of these species. It presents the characteristic wren profile of a plump, rounded body, a slender, slightly curved beak, and a long tail often held cocked upward or over the back. This wren is a rich reddish-brown on the upperparts and a warm tan below, and it has a white eyebrow over each eye. Perky and noisy, the Carolina wren hops and flits through underbrush as it calls and scolds.

Both the CAROLINA CHICKADEE and TUFTED TITMOUSE are studies in black, white, and gray, but fortunately each of them has a distinctive field mark. The chickadee is the smaller of the two, and it has a gray back, lighter underparts with a faint buffy wash over the flanks, white cheeks, a black crown, and a triangular black bib. The titmouse stands more upright and has a gray back and lighter underparts (also with buffy flanks). But it has an erect crest atop the head, while lacking the black crown and bib of the chickadee.

Three of the woodland birds are primarily winter residents. The ruby-crowned kinglet, the orange-crowned warbler, and the yellow-rumped warbler (formerly called the myrtle warbler) move into the Houston area in mid-October and stay to mid-April. On occasion I have seen the kinglet and the yellow-rumped become quite numerous in a given location.

The RUBY-CROWNED KINGLET is a small, drab bird that frequently flicks its wings and tail while foraging amid the foliage of trees. To identify it, look for a stumpy bird that is dull olive-green over the upperparts, with lighter underparts, and that has two white wing bars and a a broken white eye-ring. The male has a bright red spot on the crown, but it is not visible unless the crown feathers get ruffled by the wind; most of the time you won't see the ruby crown.

The ORANGE-CROWNED WARBLER is one of the least attractive birds you will see in the city. It is dull olive-green over the back and olive-yellow below and is devoid of field marks. This bird is distinctive by its lack of distinction. Of these seven birds of city woodlands, you will probably see the orange-crowned warbler the least. I doubt you'll ever complain.

The YELLOW-RUMPED WARBLER offers a bit more

flashiness than the orange-crowned, but not much. In its breeding plumage, seen only in its summertime range in the North, this bird is a beautiful collage of black and white and yellow. But for its winter plumage, which we see in Houston, it turns a drab, streaky brown over most of the body. Fortunately, the winter coloration retains the bright yellow rump of the breeding plumage. The rump is concealed until the bird flicks its wings open while foraging.

The BLUE-GRAY GNATCATCHER is an attractive bird that is most common in the Houston area from August through April. Like the other species, it inhabits woodlands, either dense or open, and it often shows a preference for the end of a tree branch for its foraging. It will, however, occasionally work thickets and shrubbery of the understory.

The male gnatcatcher is steely blue with light underparts, a slim beak, and a long tail that has white outer tail feathers. The female is more gray than the blue-dominated male. Both sexes have a narrow white eye-ring.

The gnatcatcher cocks its long tail up and down for balance as it meanders through the foliage looking for insects. Occasionally you can observe the white underside of the tail.

None of these woodland birds will be as conspicuous as many of the other urban birds. With practice, however, you will become adept at detecting motion in the trees and following the bird with your binoculars. Once you learn to see and track the bird, allowing yourself a good if brief look at it, you will realize that these woodland species are not as difficult to distinguish as you first thought. Above all, they are worth the effort. They are fun to watch at all times of the year, and a kinglet or gnatcatcher or yellow-rumped warbler hopping around the branches adds a hopeful touch of life to a leafless tree set against the gray winter sky.

CAROLINA WREN

Thryothorus ludovicianus

Field Marks:	6 in., reddish-brown back, tan underparts, white eyebrow, long, cocked-up tail
Habitat:	underbrush and thickets of woodlands and woodland edges
Occurrence:	all year
Behavior:	noisy, active

40. Carolina Wren
 On nest

CAROLINA CHICKADEE

Parus carolinensis

Field Marks: 4–5 in., gray back, light underparts with buffy flanks, black crown, white cheeks, triangular black bib

Habitat: forests, woodlands and their edges, wooded parks and neighborhoods

Occurrence: all year

Behavior: forages over tree branches

41. *Carolina Chickadee*
Young bird

TUFTED TITMOUSE

Parus bicolor

Field Marks: 4 1/2–5 1/2 in., upright posture, gray over
                back, lighter undersides with buffy flanks,
                erect gray crest
Habitat: woodlands and forests, wooded parks and
                neighborhoods
Occurrence: all year
Behavior: forages over tree branches

42. Tufted Titmouse

Regulus calendula

Field Marks:	4 in., small size, dull olive-green upperparts, lighter below, two white wing bars, broken white eye-ring, red crown of male sometimes visible
Habitat:	woodlands, forests, wooded areas
Occurrence:	mid-October to mid-April
Behavior:	very active foraging over tree branches, continually flits wings

43. *Ruby-crowned Kinglet (male)*

ORANGE-CROWNED

WARBLER

Vermivora celata

Field Marks:	4–5 in., uniformly drab olive-green with more yellow on underparts, no other distinguishing field marks
Habitat:	woodlands and forests, thickets
Occurrence:	mid-October to mid-April
Behavior:	forages over tree branches

44. Orange-crowned Warbler

YELLOW-RUMPED

WARBLER

Dendroica coronata

Field Marks:	5–6 in., dull gray-brown streaking over back and flanks, bright yellow rump visible when wings spread
Habitat:	woodlands, trees in parks and neighborhoods
Occurrence:	mid-October to mid-April
Behavior:	forages over tree branches

45. Yellow-rumped Warbler

BLUE-GRAY

GNATCATCHER

Polioptila caerulea

Field Marks:	4 1/2 in., male a subdued metallic blue-gray; female duller and grayer; long tail with white outer feathers in both sexes
Habitat:	woodland trees, brushy understory
Occurrence:	August through April
Behavior:	forages over tree branches, holds tail at various angles

46. Blue-gray Gnatcatcher (male)
   Captured for banding; shows small size

HERONS AND
EGRETS

Two species of egrets and two species of herons regularly inhabit Houston; in the community of forest and grassland birds most often found throughout the big city, these long-legged wading birds stand out as exotic relatives from out-of-town.

Both the great egret and the cattle egret have completely white plumage. From a distance the two are best distinguished by size. At about forty inches in length, the tall, slender great egret is almost double the size of the stocky, compact cattle egret.

The GREAT EGRET prefers wet areas around the city, such as flooded fields, the edges of ponds and lakes, and the banks of creeks and bayous. This egret has a long, slender neck that is usually held in an S shape, a yellow beak, and long black legs and feet.

The CATTLE EGRET forages in pastures or grassy areas, frequently but not always with cattle; it feeds on the grasshoppers and other insects that the cattle flush up from the grass. The bird has a short yellow beak and short yellow-brown legs. In the spring both sexes of the cattle egret develop a buff color over the chest and nape as nuptial plumage; the rest of the year the plumage is all white.

Each in its unique way, the great egret and the cattle egret tell success stories. The great egret has struggled back from the brink of extirpation in this country, to which it was pushed at gunpoint by plume hunters around the turn of the century. Today the great egret is a gloriously common bird, especially along the coast, and it serves as the symbol of the National Audubon Society. A classic image of Texas bird life is a great egret standing in a pond, its statuesque profile motionless over the water as it waits to strike a fish.

Unlike the house sparrow and starling, which were introduced to this country intentionally, the cattle egret found its way to the New World by a natural dispersion. Originally from the tropical and subtropical regions of Africa and Eurasia, the cattle egret was first recorded in Texas in 1955. From fewer than two dozen adults by the end of that decade, the cattle egret has grown to a population today of uncounted thousands throughout the state, especially along the upper coast.

I can always tell when the yellow-crowned night herons have returned to town for their annual summer visit, even before I see one myself. Around April I start to receive letters and phone calls from people grimly describing "huge, strange birds" high up in the trees, with "plumes and stripes and weird colors. . . ." Invariably the perplexed citizens are describing a YELLOW-CROWNED NIGHT-HERON.

This colorful bird roosts high in tall trees and feeds on crayfish, frogs, and insects throughout the city's creeks and bayous. It is two feet in length, and it has an upright posture. The beak is short and heavy. The bird is gray overall, except for the black head, which has a white crown and white cheek stripes. The forehead has a faint wash of yellow, giving the bird its name—in the true spirit of naming birds after their least noticeable field mark. The yellow-crowned night heron is the most tropical-looking of all the long-legged wading birds encountered in the city.

The most secretive of this group, as well as the smallest,

is the GREEN-BACKED HERON. This little crow-sized heron will most often be seen when flushed out of dense vegetation bordering a creek or bayou. The bird doesn't usually feed out in the open in the manner of other herons and egrets; it skulks through willows and reeds, searching quietly for fish, crayfish, and dragonflies.

The green-backed heron is a dark bird overall, with a subdued gray-green back, a chestnut head and neck, and a narrow white stripe down the throat and chest. The heavy beak appears long in proportion to the bird's head.

In flight it moves aloft on steady, powerful wingbeats; its wings have a downward-curved look about them; this flight profile and the small size and dark color serve in identifying the green-backed heron from a distance.

GREAT EGRET

Casmerodius albus

Field Marks:	37–41 in., all white, long slender neck, yellow beak, black legs and feet
Habitat:	ponds, creeks, swamps, wet fields, pastures
Occurrence:	all year
Behavior:	stands motionless by water, waiting for fish

47. *Great Egret*

CATTLE EGRET

Bubulcus ibis

Field Marks:	19–21 in., all white except for buffy head and chest during spring, short yellow beak, pale yellow-orange legs
Habitat:	dry fields and pastures, open grassy areas
Occurrence:	all year
Behavior:	often in large flocks with grazing cattle

48. Cattle Egret

YELLOW-CROWNED
NIGHT-HERON
Nyctanassa violacea

Field Marks:	22–28 in., gray body, upright posture, short stout beak, black head with white crown and cheek stripe, faint yellow forehead
Habitat:	creeks, streams, and bayous for feeding, roosts high in tall trees
Occurrence:	April through September
Behavior:	solitary, stands quietly by water

49. Yellow-crowned Night-Heron

GREEN-BACKED HERON

Butorides striatus

Field Marks: 15–22 in., small and dark, gray-green
back, chestnut head and neck, yellow legs,
long stout beak

Habitat: dense vegetation along creeks and bayous

Occurrence: March through October

Behavior: secretive, usually seen when flushed

50. Green-backed Heron

American Robin

I once jokingly asked professional bird-watcher Ben Feltner if the formal name of the robin should really be "robin red-breast." "No," he said, mock-solemnly, "friendly robin red-breast." Regardless of what you call this popular bird, everyone recognizes the AMERICAN ROBIN by its rich, brick-red breast and belly. Its back is gray-brown, its head is black, and its slender, pointed beak is yellow with a black tip. A broken white eye-ring surrounds each eye.

Often in large flocks, robins congregate on lawns and on the grassy embankments of bayous, parks, and fields. They frequently feed on the ground, searching out earthworms, berries, grains, and insects.

In other parts of the country the robin is celebrated as a bird of spring, but in southeast Texas it is a harbinger of the deep winter. The bird starts moving into the Houston area in large numbers in December, and it remains fairly numerous through March. Robins begin to migrate back north in April, and by late summer they are seldom seen in the city. There have been years, however, during which they have been rather scarce in the winter, possibly due to a shortage of food.

Once in a while you will see a straggler remain through the year. There was a solitary robin that lived year-round near the main entrance of Rice University a few years back. It hopped amid the shadows of the great pines, nipping here and there for earthworms under the litter of pine needles. When it would reach the old sidewalk, cracked with the uplifting roots of the live oaks arching over Main Street, it darted back amid the trees.

AMERICAN ROBIN

Turdus migratorius

Field Marks:	9–11 in., brick-red breast, gray-brown back, black head, broken white eye-ring, yellow beak with black tip
Habitat:	open grassy areas, trees
Occurrence:	December through March
Behavior:	often gathers in large flocks to feed in open areas

51. American Robin

Lesser Snow Goose

The LESSER SNOW GOOSE arrives in Texas in October and announces the coming of winter with its plaintive honking high in the quickening fall air. Often the first snow geese of the season will only be heard through the darkness over the city as they move south to settle on the coastal plain. You may see them in the late afternoon as they fly in their trademark V formation, the long, ragged trails slowly undulating behind the leader at the tip. Or your first view may be a field of geese on the Katy Prairie, brilliant white against the winter brown of the grain stubble and plowed earth.

Snow geese are among the easiest of local birds to identify, which is fortunate since they will usually be seen only at great distances. The snow goose is all white, with black wingtips. If you can get close, you can see the pink bill with the black crescent along each side, giving the bird a mischievous smiling appearance.

Among the all-white geese there will also be some unusual geese with irregular dark patches. The "blue goose," as this variety of snow goose is informally known, belongs to the same species but is a different color phase. The head of the blue goose is usually white; the body has varying amounts of white and dark brown on the chest, neck, back, and wings.

The slightly larger greater snow goose nests around Baffin Bay and winters along the mid-Atlantic coast; the lesser snow goose breeds on the high tundra across central and western Canada and winters along the Pacific and Gulf coasts.

LESSER SNOW GOOSE

Chen caerulescens

Field Marks:	28 in., white plumage, black wingtips visible in flight, pink beak with dark "smiling" patch, dark color phase marked by dark back and chest, white head
Habitat:	large fields on coastal prairie
Occurrence:	October through March
Behavior:	usually in huge flocks, flies in V formation

52. Lesser Snow Goose
  White and dark forms

Turkey Vulture

Few people like the TURKEY VULTURE, and this is unfortunate but understandable. What else would you expect people to think about a big, black, ugly bird with a bare fleshy head that gorges on dead animals in the road, and, when it isn't doing that, just sits around waiting for something to die? This is the image that most of us have of the "buzzard," and it is an incomplete one. This well-known carrion eater, the most widespread of the New World vultures, is an outstanding flier, has a sense of smell possessed by few other birds, and occupies an important—although unglamorous—niche in the food chain.

The turkey vulture is a large, black-brown bird that is widespread throughout the state and is often seen within the city. On hot, bright days it soars high in the air in search of carrion. While in flight it displays two important field marks: a broad band of pale feathers along the trailing edge of the six-foot wingspan and a long, narrow tail.

The bird soars and glides on outstretched wings for great distances on thermal updrafts. It holds its wings back in a shallow V while soaring, and frequently tilts back and forth while aloft. Vultures often feed and roost in groups of a dozen or more individuals, but it is not unusual to see a single vulture on the wing or feasting on a roadside kill.

The featherless head, also present on Old World vultures, is believed to be an adaptation for carrion-eaters. A vulture sticking its head into a carcass will get it messy; a bare head stays cleaner more readily than a feathered one.

TURKEY VULTURE

Cathartes aura

Field Marks: 26–32 in., pink fleshy head, long narrow wings with pale flight feathers, long narrow tail

Habitat: open rural areas, often seen over fields within city

Occurrence: all year

Behavior: soars high for long periods with few wingbeats, often seen feeding, gliding, or roosting in groups

53. Turkey Vulture

OWLS

The two most common owls seen within the city are the EASTERN SCREECH-OWL and the BARN OWL. As nocturnal hunters that roost in seclusion during the day, the owls will not be encountered frequently (unless you are lucky enough to have one roosting in a tree in your yard). Owls have long fascinated us with their secretive ways and omniscient demeanor. They are in fact powerful and efficient predators who are endowed with a sharp sense of hearing and who can fly silently on softened feathers, dodging tree limbs and branches, toward their unsuspecting prey.

At seven to ten inches long, the screech-owl is the smaller of the two, and its appearance suggests a miniature great horned owl. This stumpy, compact little raptor has two color phases, a reddish-brown phase and the more common gray phase. In either color the bird is heavily streaked over the front and back. A pair of small ear tufts sits atop the head, over a broad face with large yellow eyes.

The screech-owl is widespread throughout the Houston area. It can inhabit open woodlands, forested areas, parks, neighborhoods, and agricultural regions. The screech-owl does not "screech" but calls with a haunting tremolo that ascends and then descends in pitch.

Even among a group of such distinction as the owls, the barn owl stands out with its ghostly, brooding presence. This tall, leggy bird is pale on its underparts and wing linings and is light brown over its back and face. The trademark facial disc is roughly heart-shaped; the eyes are dark.

The barn owl is not as common within the city as the screech-owl. It is widespread throughout the state, however, and is found in most parts of the state except for densely forested regions.

Both owls roost during the day in the hollows of tree trunks, amid heavy foliage, or, in the case of the barn owl, in barns or outlying, unoccupied farm buildings. At twilight they venture forth to hunt. Owls hunt by their extremely sharp sense of hearing as well as by their excellent eyesight. The rustle in the grass of a field mouse or lizard will bring the bird swooping down to attack. Owls kill prey with their powerful talons, then tear it up with their hooked beaks.

The large, flattened eyes of the owls adapt the birds to conditions of low light, but their shape makes it impossible for the eyes to rotate in their sockets. To compensate for the immobility of the eye, the owls have evolved a very flexible neck that allows a wide range of rotation of the head for peripheral vision.

Unless you are lucky enough just to come upon an owl, you can expect some difficulty in seeing one. A reliable way to find owls is to join one of the periodic owl-watching trips offered by a local nature organization. On these excursions you frequently see not only the barn owl and screech-owl but also the barred owl and great horned owl. Experienced observers on these trips know where the owls are and summon them with squeaks and owl calls for observation in a spotlight.

EASTERN SCREECH-OWL

Otus asio

Field Marks:	7–10 in., small with ear tufts, heavy streaking in either gray or reddish-brown
Habitat:	wooded areas, neighborhood trees, open areas with stands of trees
Occurrence:	all year
Behavior:	roosts secretively by day, hunts at night

BARN OWL

Tyto alba

Field Marks:	16 in., tall and upright, pale below, light brown over back and head, heart-shaped face
Habitat:	wooded areas, old abandoned farm buildings
Occurrence:	October through April
Behavior:	roosts secretively by day, hunts at night

54. *Eastern Screech-Owl (red phase)*

55. Eastern Screech-Owl (gray phase)

56. *Barn Owl*

Ruby-throated Hummingbird

Most of the sixteen species of hummingbirds that occur regularly in the United States inhabit the western part of the country. The only hummingbird to range throughout the eastern states is the RUBY-THROATED HUMMINGBIRD. While at least five other species of hummingbirds spend the winter in southeast Texas, the colorful, energetic ruby-throated hummingbird is by far the most common one seen in Houston.

The ruby-throated displays male and female plumages; both are iridescent green over the back and crown, while the male has a brilliant ruby-red gorget (large patch over the throat). The female's throat is white like the rest of her underparts. The male's tail is dark and deeply forked, while the female's tail is rounded and tipped with white on the outer tail feathers. The bird reaches almost four inches in length.

Although hummingbirds are the smallest members of the bird world, they are among its most powerful and acrobatic fliers. Hummingbirds can rotate their wings forward or backward, which no other bird can do; this allows them to fly forward or backward and to hover in place in midair.

You will most often see a ruby-throated as it races through your yard on blurred wings, hovering around a bush here, a flower bed there, then sailing off to another yard, constantly searching for red flowers, such as Turk's cap and trumpet creeper, on which to feed. The ruby-throated hummingbird has, like most other hummers, a long, slender beak, which the bird pokes down into flowers to draw out nectar with its long, protrusible tongue.

Ruby-throated hummingbirds have a dual migratory season in the Houston area. They are common from mid-March to mid-May, become scarce for a few months, then become common again from mid-July to mid-October before becoming scarce until the following spring.

RUBY-THROATED

HUMMINGBIRD

Archilochus colubris

Field Marks:	3–3 1/2 in., small size, iridescent green over back and white on chest and belly in both sexes; male has brilliant ruby-red throat and dark forked tail; female has white throat and rounded tail with white-tipped outer tail feathers
Habitat:	yards, fields, parks where flowers are plentiful
Occurrence:	mid-March to mid-May, mid-July to mid-October
Behavior:	rapid, intense, hovering flight, attracted to hummingbird feeders

57. Ruby-throated Hummingbird (male)
Note: red of throat shows only in light from proper direction

Scissor-tailed Flycatcher

Among the many things for which the good people of the great state of Oklahoma should be thankful is their state bird—the SCISSOR-TAILED FLYCATCHER. This beautiful bird migrates into the Houston area in spring and stays through the summer into fall. It is a bird of the open country, where it perches on power lines, fences, and exposed branches to watch for the flying insect life on which it feeds.

The scissor-tailed flycatcher is a slender, graceful bird that is pale gray over the back and head and whitish over its underparts. The flanks and belly are washed with pale pink. The key field mark for the flycatcher is a very long, deeply forked black-and-white tail. Females are slightly smaller and duller than males; immature scissor-taileds have a much shorter tail. When the bird is at rest the tail appears solid in structure, but in flight the flycatcher frequently spreads its tail, revealing the deep split.

Like the other flycatchers, the scissor-tailed feeds by first watching from a perch in an open vantage point. When it sees a flying insect, it flies up, grabs it, and then returns to the perch.

In the city the scissor-tailed flycatcher often rests on power lines and fences near open areas like grassy fields and pastures. The bird starts to move into the area in mid-March and is abundant until mid-October.

SCISSOR-TAILED

FLYCATCHER

Tyrannus forficatus

Field Marks: 12–15 in., graceful bird with very long
tail, pale gray back and head, whitish
underparts with faint pink flanks and belly

Habitat: open country, pastures, fields,

Occurrence: mid-March to mid-October

Behavior: usually perches on power line or other
high exposed perch, flies off to catch
insects and then returns to perch

58. Scissor-tailed Flycatcher

Barn Swallow

The swallows are a group of graceful, acrobatic birds who fly in great, rapid sweeps over open fields to feed upon flying insects. Three species migrate in spring and fall to the rural areas outside Houston: the barn swallow, the tree swallow and the cliff swallow. Of these, the barn swallow is most often observed in large fields and open areas around the city.

The BARN SWALLOW is deep iridescent blue-black over the back and wings, the color of a shiny shotgun barrel. In the male the chest is a rich buff brown and the throat and forehead are a darker chestnut brown. In the female these colors are somewhat lighter. The long tail is deeply forked, more so than in any other American swallow.

Barn swallows are usually observed in large flocks over a field or in the vicinity of an overpass, under which they build their cuplike nests of mud. They are often accompanied in flight over fields by the smaller tree swallow, which has bright white underparts and a shorter, notched tail.

The best field marks for either of these swallows are the color of the underparts and the length and shape of the tail. In spring and fall migration the barn swallow can become abundant over the fields and pastures of the coastal prairie.

The cliff swallow nests with barn swallows beneath underpasses outside the city, and the two birds will often be seen flying together near their nests. The cliff swallow has a stubby, squared-off tail with a conspicuous buff patch on the rump.

BARN SWALLOW

Hirundo rustica

Field Marks:	7 in., deep metallic blue-black over back, buff chest, chestnut throat and forehead, long deeply forked tail
Habitat:	open areas, pastures and fields
Occurrence:	late March through May and September through October
Behavior:	rapid, sweeping flight in flocks

59. *Barn Swallow*

Eastern Bluebird

Of all the birds that I remember identifying for the first time, the EASTERN BLUEBIRD stands out as vividly as any of them. During my early birdwatching days years ago, I was in Montgomery County with some friends on a bright winter day when we sighted a bird perched on a power line. Its plumage was brilliant in the bright sunlight; we had never before seen such a striking mix of colors. A rich, warm brown throat and chest was set off by the bold electric blue of the head, back, tail, and wings. He sat there for a while and then flew. All of us realized that we would never forget our first bluebird.

We were observing a male eastern bluebird, the more brightly colored of the two sexes. In addition to the brown and blue, its belly was clean white. The color pattern is similar in the female, but the colors are less intense, with more gray throughout.

This small, attractive bird is a winter resident in southeast Texas, although it may linger there throughout the summer in lower numbers. Bluebirds are most common from late September to mid-March.

Eastern bluebirds occupy a wide variety of habitats, such as semi-open woodlands, rural areas, prairies and pastures, orchards, and residential areas, as well as along fence rows and roadways. They often perch out in the open on tree branches or power lines. Bluebirds nest in cavities, and bluebird boxes are popular in some of the northern states where bluebird numbers have declined in recent years.

EASTERN BLUEBIRD

Sialia sialis

Field Marks: 6 in., bright blue upperparts, chestnut chest and throat, white belly; female duller and grayer

Habitat: open areas with trees, farmlands, parks, neighborhoods, woodland edges and clearings

Occurrence: late September to mid-March

Behavior: perches in trees and on power lines

60. Eastern Bluebird (male)

61. Eastern Bluebird (female)

Brown Thrasher

If you ever see a large brown bird with a long tail and a heavily streaked breast thrashing around on the ground among the bushes and trees in your back yard, you most likely have seen a BROWN THRASHER. This well-named bird visits the Houston area each winter, from October through April; it adds a touch of life to the winter woods.

The thrasher is reddish-brown on the crown, back, wings, and tail, and the face is dull gray. It has a fairly long, heavy beak and yellow eyes. The wings have two white wing bars. The underparts are light, with heavy dark brown streaking, and the sides of the breast and belly are lighter brown.

Although they will forage in trees, brown thrashers often forage on or near the ground in thickets and amid dense growth of bushes and shrubbery. The thrasher hops around, rustling through the foliage, rooting its beak through the leaves and grass, looking for bugs and worms.

The bird flies near the ground as it moves from thicket to thicket through the woods and residential yards. It flies for great distances only during migration; most of the time it confines its flight to short trips among bushes, trees, and shrubs.

BROWN THRASHER

Toxostoma rufum

Field Marks:	12 in., brown back, crown, and wings, whitish underparts with heavy brown streaks, long tail, gray-brown face
Habitat:	wooded areas with undergrowth, shrubs, bushes
Occurrence:	October through April
Behavior:	feeds on ground among forest undergrowth and shrubbery

62. Brown Thrasher

Brown Creeper

You will probably see the BROWN CREEPER the least often of any of the urban birds in this book. The brown creeper is not particularly rare or uncommon, but it is a shy little bird whose dull plumage allows it to blend in well with its surroundings.

The slim, compact brown creeper has brown upperparts that are mottled and streaked with gray and white. The underparts are lighter, and the undertail and flanks have a buffy wash to them. The bird has a long, slender beak, a long, stiff tail, and large, grasping feet.

Like the nuthatches and woodpeckers, the creeper moves up and down tree trunks in search of insects dwelling beneath the bark. The bird usually begins at or near the base of a tree trunk and slowly works its way upward in a spiral fashion, probing and digging into the bark with its beak. The rigid tail serves as a support for the bird as it makes its way up a trunk.

When the creeper reaches the top, it will fly downward toward the next tree, land near the base, and begin to work its way up again. If observed in flight, the creeper will be making these short hops from tree to tree in its strong, straight flight. But most often the creeper will be seen creeping up a tree trunk. Since the bird is so well camouflaged by its dark brown, mottled plumage, your best chance to see one is during a walk in the woods or in your back yard when you simply come across it. Or if you see a bird make a strong, direct flight across the open toward a tree trunk and land right on it, you may be observing this interesting bird. Learn to distinguish it from the woodpeckers, most of which are more boldly patterned and larger than the brown creeper.

BROWN CREEPER

Certhia americana

Field Marks:	5–6 in., dull-colored with slender curved beak, long stiff tail, light underparts, back mottled and streaked with brown, white, and gray
Habitat:	trees in woodlands, neighborhood parks, along creek beds
Occurrence:	late October through early April
Behavior:	solitary, crawls up tree trunks, well camouflaged

63. Brown Creeper